Some quick thoughts from those Doug has spoken to or taught:

Doug is a dynamic and energetic speaker who leaves you feeling that
you can have great success.
Carla Young www.tangentideas.com

The tips for success, and the hands-on approach to Douglas' coaching methods are unsurpassed. Doug has an energy and effervescence that is nothing short of contagious. I am more sure of success now, than I ever was before due to his reassurance and guidance.
Kathleen Johnson, Reflections Image management

"His smile, manner, and pleasant inquisitive personality make him one others desire to be around. His confidence and enthusiasm indicate he has strong leadership characteristics. "
Doug Stutz – Continuing Education, Brigham Young University Idaho.

"The very best instructor we ever had to work with our teachers."
Yi Ping, Xin Zhou No.1 School, China

You are my second best teacher, because you taught me that I am my first best teacher.
Wang Yuan – Chinese Teacher

Doug is naturally at ease in talking to people, including children and seniors, and his manner puts his audience at ease as well. We have had many positive comments.
Howard Snyder, Alberta Community Development

I found him to be a dynamic individual with a genuine love for teaching. He is gifted. His students love him and he has a unique way of connecting with them. Doug knows how to bring out the best in those around him.
Sherri Lewis – GTC instructor

I have learned many useful things from Doug. In fact, I didn't like my school before I heard him. But since then I learned that I should I shouldn't wait for happiness but it's up to me to find it. His lessons were very lively and interesting.
-Bonnie Jia, Chinese Student, Da Tong, Shanxi Province

Thank you for your wonderful presentations. I have never met such an excellent person before. You are the first I had such an inspiration from.

Han Jiao Jiao – Chinese Student, Xin Zhou, Shanxi Province

I have decided to study harder so that I can make a lot of money in the future. At that time I will then fly to Canada to find you and tell you that's it's you who has encouraged me to study so hard.

Lu Xia Yu – Chinese Student, Suo Zhou, Shanxi Province

I have never seen a more wonderful teacher.

Liu Yan – Chinese Teacher, Wu Tai Shan, Shanxi Province

You make it easy to dream.

Yang RongFang – Chinese Student

Thank you for showing us what it means to have a beautiful day and to never let it get away.
Duan Lijuan – Chinese Student

I have been a very shy person who didn't believe there was much for me. But when I met you things began to change. Happiness is not something we should wait for, but we should go and catch it. And the more I started looking for it – the more I now find.
Zheng Rui Qin – Chinese Student, Wu Tai, Shan Xi Province

You have given me great courage to work harder and get through difficulties in my life.
Wang Jian Fei – Chinese Student

Your teachings will stay with me forever in my heart.
Zhang Hao – Chinese Student

Your words have stayed with me.
"The Sun of tomorrow is always Brighter! And it will be a beautiful day!"
Luo GongBin – Chinese Teacher

———————————————————————————

I believe it will be impossible to ever have another person in my life teach me so much.
Li Yan – Chinese Teacher

———————————————————————————

I think that I can not forget you forever.
Li Tong Mao – Chinese Student

———————————————————————————

Our life has become colourful because of you. Do you remember me?
I gave you a silkworm to eat. Was it delicious?
Zha Qiang – Chinese Student

All I can say is that you have changed my life.
Sun Jing Jao Chinese Student

––––––––––––––––––––––––––––

Our time together is one of the most important memories in my life.
Kand Xzao Long – Chinese Student

––––––––––––––––––––––––––––

Great Douglas!
Funny Douglas!
Best Douglas!
Forever Douglas!
Wang Lei – Chinese Student

––––––––––––––––––––––––––––

You taught us that nothing could stand in our way!
You taught us that by contributing to the world it will be amazing.
Douglas You are Superman!
Li Jie, Chinese Student

Sometimes I get into trouble. But I now understand that I have power to choose differently.
Hao Ting Ting Chinese Student

Your contribution was Valuable and helped to foster the spirit of Personal development, dialogue and discovery for which the symposium exists. I trust that you found your involvement also worthwhile and encourage you to consider participating with us again, if your situation permits. –
Dr. Joseph B. Romney Ricks College Honors Program
(Issues and Interactions symposium)

365 Daily lessons from

AMAZING
SUCCESS

By Douglas Vermeeren

365 Daily Lessons from Amazing Success
Copyright © 2007 Douglas J. Vermeeren

ISBN – 978-0-9782725-1-7

Printed in Canada

AMAZING
SUCCESS

<u>**Ordering Information**</u>

Quantity Book Sales. Special discounts are available on quantity purchases by corporations, associations, educational groups and others. For details contact the special sales department at the Business Boost Offices.

Orders for bookstores and wholesales please contact the publisher by the above e-mail.

Fund raising organizations, coaches and trainers – please contact us to discuss how you can use this book to your advantage for additional income opportunities.

Business Boost Success books department may be contacted by e-mail at: Books@BusinessBoostSuccess.com
www.BusinessBoostSuccess.com

This book is dedicated to my brothers who are very amazing people.

I have to also give a super special thanks to my beautiful wife Holly.

Without her help, patience, (I should actually mention her patience twice)
Her love, forgiveness, kindness, inspiration and faith in me,
this book would never have been Possible.

Introduction

It is a Wednesday afternoon in December. I have just finished reviewing and compiling my final notes for this volume. It has been an interesting journey meeting and interviewing what I consider to be some of the most successful people on the planet. I have met celebrities, political leaders, religious leaders, financial hot shots and others.

No doubt these people are leaving a great impact on many around them.

It is their attributes and lessons which led to the creation of this book and its sister volume, "Amazing Success – Lessons from the most successful people I know. "

This book is slightly different than the other in a few ways. Firstly, this book contains no interviews. Nor does it teach, or explain the principles and individual lessons from the other book. Instead, it shares some instant daily applications and things for you to consider right now in your journey towards being more successful.

When I started collecting the lessons that made up the companion volume to this book, "Amazing Success" this book began to take shape in the back of my mind.

Each entry is brief for several reasons. Firstly, I wanted this book to be easy to apply and give you power instantly. These bite sized lesson can make a dramatic difference for you without you having to invest a lot of time to master them.

Secondly, I wanted to make the book in such a way that you could flip open almost anywhere, even with a spare second, and find a thought that could be developed into instant action. If you are like me, you have found comfort in the past of just flipping a book open in a random way and quickly reaping something useful.

I am confident that these brief, point style lessons will make a difference for you. I also invite you to go back and read the complete book "Amazing Success" as often as your circumstances will allow you to. Those lessons will help you see these little lessons for what they really are.

I have also included the transcript from a radio recent interview that I did about the "Amazing Possibilities" books. I do so to give you a little bit of background on the project and to give you a better context for the following 365 points. Hopefully you will find it interesting and helpful on your journey to success.

Wishing you success and Amazing Achievement,

Douglas Vermeeren

Amazing Possibilities Interview

This is the modified text from an interview done on California 103FM radio. The interviewer questions and comments are in bold print, while Doug's answers and responses are printed along side.

Interviewer: I am here today in the Studio with Douglas Vermeeren. Doug is one of the top business and personal success speakers in the world today.

He has taught, trained and motivated groups in the U.S., Canada, Europe and through out China. While in China he was given the distinction of Visiting Professor by the Wu Zhai University.

Spending a full year there he taught more than 3500 leaders, teachers and students each week in a variety of cities. He was the only North American to ever speak at the Teachers Day conference to political and educational leaders in communist China. His remarks received ovations and were translated and distributed to multiple newspapers across the nation and 4000 other leaders and government officials.

In December of 1995 Avenue Magazine featured Doug as one of the Top Ten Calgarians to watch.

In 2003, Doug created the "Jump Start your teenager" series which was featured on CFCN television and presented in several schools across Canada.

Doug has also written several books and multiple articles. (Several of which have been translated into more than 22 languages worldwide.)

Thanks for joining us in the Studio today Doug.

Doug: Thanks for having me.

Interviewer: Tell us a little bit your new project Amazing Success – Lessons from the most success people I know.

Doug: It's all about learning how to turn human potential into amazing and awesome performance. These particular lessons came from interviews with almost 400 top achievers from all over the world. And then I took these lessons and broke them down into principles that are easy to understand and apply.

Interviewer: How did you come with the idea for the book?

Doug: Over the past several years I have had the chance to travel and live all over the world. I spent over two years in Europe – spending time in France, Belgium, Luxembourg, Holland and Germany. I spent time in a variety of places in the United States and Canada and then most recently spent a full year in China. I had a chance to meet several different kinds of people. Some of them were quite successful, some famous, some very wealthy. And of course there were many that were quite the opposite.

I have been keeping a daily journal for more than a decade or so and one day I was reading my entries and noticed that I had made similar remarks about a few of the successful people I had met. It was then that the thought really struck me. There must be a formula for why some people are successful and others not. I then began to read all materials that I could get my hands on and interview as many successful people as I could find.

By the time I was finished I had observed and spoken with more than 400 people in more than two dozen countries from around the world. And from that experience I found 12 common traits from top achievers. These will lead anyone to truly amazing possibilities.

Interviewer: You say that anyone can attain success what do you mean by that?

Doug: I mean exactly that. Anyone can apply these principles. You don't have to be rich to get rich. You don't have to be involved in big business to get involved in big business. I have seen these principles literally change lives. The only real attributes a person needs to begin this process are a desire to do it and a determination to do it.

The challenge with most people is they give up too easy. They are conditioned to believe they will fail and so they self sabotage themselves before they even really get started.

Interviewer: One thing I found interesting was your definition of Success. Can you tell us more about that?

Doug: Well, I would prefer to start with what success is not. I'd like to share a definition that found not to long ago in a dictionary.

The definition read: *"Success – the accomplishment of what is desired or aimed at. Achievement. Attainment of wealth or fame. A person or thing which succeeds. To attain a desired end.*

There are a few problems that I have with that definition.

1. Success is not just the accomplishment of a desire, but the continual series of accomplishments. Success is really a habit, not an event.

2. Wealth and fame do not equal success. I have met many people who had these two elements and they were unbalanced and not happy.

   While it is true that these two things can be fruits of success, they are really not measurements of it.

   For example when I was in China I visited the world famous Wu Tai Mountain. It is also known as the very birth place of Buddhism. While there I had an opportunity to visit several monasteries, nun convents and other locations populated by Buddhists monks. It was incredible and enlightening. As I interacted with them I found that they possessed many of the same attributes as other top achievers I had met – but they had no enormous wealth or fame. They had prosperity. Which is different.

   In contrast while living in California I was often surrounded by many who did have wealth and fame through the film and television industry, but many of these individuals led such an unbalanced lifestyle that they lacked many of the attributes of the other happy and successful people I had met.

Prosperity and abundance are a part of a person – they are attributes. They have more to do with how a person thinks, performs and their habits. Financial wealth can be numbers on a bank statement. Someone can be wealthy without having abundance. Strive for the greater.

3. Lastly, success is not an end. All the successful people were not at their end. They were alive, well and in some cases many of them would dispute that rather than being at the end of their journey they were just entering the beginning.

Interviewer: Very interesting. So what is Success?

Doug: Success is a continual journey towards prosperity, self improvement and happiness. It allows us to create Amazing Possibilities!

Interviewer: What do you mean by Amazing Possibilities?

Doug: Amazing possibilities is about opening as many doors as you can in your life. Creating new opportunities and allowing for exciting experiences. It is literally creating Amazing Possibilities in you life! As I observed those who applied the Success lessons it was clear that they consistently produced Amazing things in their own lives. What you put in is exactly what you will get out.

And to get amazing results you can't just put in lots of input. You have to put in the right input. And if you put Amazing stuff in you get Amazing stuff out.

Interviewer: So what are those common principles you learned from the most successful people?

Doug: The 12 points are:

1. Build on a good foundation.
2. Have a plan and a destination
3. Get organized.
4. Avoid procrastination
5. Honest, loyal and responsible.
6. Ever present.
7. Getting with the right crowd.
8. The importance of work and play.
9. Think Big.

10. Stick to it.
11. Become a master of your money.
12. Strive for personal improvement.

Interviewer: Can you tell us a little bit about each these principles?

Doug: Well, starting with the first principle of building on a good foundation, this is really the beginning. Some authors have talked about starting with a personal mission statement or a credo of sorts. This principle is similar in some ways. However, there is a really big difference between just writing a mission statement and building on a good foundation.

Foundation is much deeper than that. It really speaks about the core values, principles and goals that drive the individual.

The second principle is Have a plan and a destination. I have always been fascinated by this principle. I have met a lot of people with destinations and no plan. Maybe you have met them before too. They want to be rich – but have no idea how to do it. Or they talk about the big new house they will own, or the new car or whatever – and they figure that things will just work out if they are supposed to.

These people don't have a plan.

On the other end of the spectrum I have also met those who have lots of plans but really no final destination. These people change where they are headed on a regular basis. Sometimes they jump from job to job or different business ideas and even relationships. They have no vision of the end.

The more we can get both of these things figured out, finding a plan and a destination, the sooner we will find ourselves on a fast track to success.

It reminds me of a quote I am sure everyone has heard. "The journey of a thousand miles begins with a single footstep?" I think that is totally wrong.

The journey of a Thousand miles begins with a single footstep alright, if you don't know where you want to go. The better way to express this quote if you wanted it to be true should be more like "The journey to where you want to go (your destination) begins with a single footstep in the right direction." That will make a big difference.

The third principle is to get organized. Organization is the key to growth. If you can't manage what you already have how can you build upon it? Being organized also breeds calmness and a self confidence that allows you to go further and dream bigger. It also allows you to implement your dreams and ideas at a quicker rate.

Fourth – Avoid Procrastination. One of my favourite sayings is that "Procrastination is the greatest thief of all time." Procrastination robs many people of time and that limits success.

Successful adults put things in priority and this doesn't always mean the path of least resistance. It means doing what needs to get done. It is also interesting to note that most average people spend an enormous amount of time and energy putting out fires that could have been prevented through preparation and action. Successful people eliminate the possibility of fire by acting instantly.

Remember everyone has the same number of hours in the day. The really big difference is in how we use them.

Fifth – Be Honest, Loyal and responsible – There is so much to discuss in this lesson, but I want to sum it up by simply stating that successful people are examples of honesty, loyalty and act responsibly. They accept responsibility for challenges when they were involved and they sort things out. They do not make excuses or pass the buck. They hung onto the buck. That's why they were successful. They find solutions. They became solutions.

Sixth - Be ever present. This includes everything in the ways successful people conduct their relationships with others. Everything from how they listen to how they make themselves available for others. And I might mention that being available all the time for everybody is not the right answer either.

To be ever present really means in some cases to not be present at all. It means to carefully select where it is best to be present. And since no one can be everywhere at once, you have got to decide. Where will you invest your time?

Seventh – Success has a lot to do with getting with the right crowd. And it isn't just about the people you surround yourself with but everything you surround yourself with.

That's right even the way you dress has a huge impact on your effectiveness. Don't believe me? Think in your mind about Halloween for a minute. When you put on a scary mask or outfit does that automatically affect your mood and how you behave towards others? Of course it does. I remember as a teenager I dressed one summer as a mascot for parks and recreation programs. The minute I put on that big racoon suit I was somebody different. The same applies to how we dress and everything else we surround ourselves with. It affects how we feel.

It is interesting to notice that success is achieved in by a team. I never once saw a successful person all alone achieving. All successful people had relationships and teams that helped them to build what they were doing.

Eighth – The Importance of work and play. You've probably heard the saying work hard, play hard. When success people work – they work hard. I saw a statistic the other day that talked about work. How much do most people work in a day? It wasn't very much.

You want to be more successful instantly? Work when it is time to work.   And when it is time to play the same thing goes, put work aside. Learn how to separate the two. Most self employed people or sales people find troubles with this. That is why so many of them burn out.

They can't separate when it's time to really work and when it's time to put work away. One of my favourite stories is about an old hunter who would unstring his bow every time he hung it up. A young man one day asked him. 'Why do you unstring the bow each time?" His response was "A bow that is constantly strung soon looses its spring." It is true with each of us.

If we are all work and no play – we soon loose our spring.

Ninth is to think Big. The bigger your thinking the bigger your possibility. It's as simple as that.

The seeds are within every human to accomplish amazing possibilities.

The challenge with most small thinkers is that they are so caught up in thinking small and being distracted by small problems that they never get anywhere.

Tenth - Stick to it.   Everything requires a germination period. It is like growing flowers. They take time to grow. And you can't get a flower growing faster by pulling on it.

Successful people stick to it. Quitting before you get to the finish line is like getting out of a boat before it reaches the shore.

Keep in mind that there is a difference between adjusting your course and giving up. Successful people do not give up - but they often readjust their plan to take advantage of new insights or overcome unseen challenges.

Eleven - Become a master of your money. Money is a tool. Nothing more, nothing less. It reminds me of my high school days when I worked in a wood shop. Craftsman created amazing wood pieces. Cabinets, mouldings counter tops, beautiful bevelled doors. Amazing things.

But while I was there I also saw less experienced people work. They were sloppy and often made a terrible mess of materials, created large amounts of waste and on two occasions I even saw people get very hurt. To the point of irreparable physical damage and missing fingers.

Money management can be the same. Those who understand the tool can build amazing things. Those who abuse or don't care don't create much and can even cause harm that is very difficult to repair.

Twelve - Continual self improvement - This is the most common attribute among leaders. Leaders are also learners.

It is interesting to me that education and self improvement are tools that are reasonably easy for most people to access, but most people don't bother.

Knowledge is power. Power, therefore, can be reasonably easy for most people to access. Education, experience and creativity are really the bricks from which all great things are built.

People with lots of money have failed. While those with great ideas have gone a long way without any money at all. Why? I think it has a lot to do with what they know and believe.

Interviewer: So who do you feel was the most successful person that you have ever met?

Doug: Without a doubt my mother. She was a stay at home mom. After she raised us, my brothers and I, she returned to the work force and is now quite successful in the dental field.

She then set out to accomplish some dreams. She had a dream to become physically fit and learn how to run. It was a lot of hard work. And discipline. But soon she was able to run a significant distance.

But that wasn't enough. She recognized amazing possibilities ahead and set a goal to run a marathon. After dedication and hard work and several months she qualified for her first marathon. She ran it with excitement and the achievement changed her life. She prepared and ran several others. She was on fire.

She became so successful she even began training with former Olympians.

Then things came crashing down one day.

Suddenly as she was running her knee gave out.

This was a fairly serious knee injury and doctors told her she needed to stop.

But she had a dream and wouldn't let anything get in her way. The doctors recommended that she rest for six months. She knew that six months would rob her of all the training and effort she had invested. So without doctor approval she began to start training again after only six weeks.

It is amazing the drive that humans can have to accomplish something when we are really motivated.

Soon as she began to run, she found that the weak knee would not cooperate.

But she decided she could not quit. She had come so far. This is a common trait of top achievers. They never quit. Sometimes they readjust their plan, but they never quit.

My mother also adjusted her plan. And as you'll see it worked out even better than she imagined.

A friend introduced her to a variation on her dream of running. This variation is called speed walking. She tried it and became immediately hooked. She decided to switched sports and began again to develop a new technique and set of skills.

It wasn't long until she had conditioned herself to be able to perform at competitive levels. To her surprise within a very short time she found herself competing at the World speed walking competition.

Remember this was a stay at home mom.

Do you want to know the result of that competition? Two silver medals. This is the world's competition. My mom took home two silver medals. She can walk faster than most people run. It's amazing. And all because she pursued her dream. Everything begins with a dream.

I am very curious to know what she will do next. I am pretty proud of her. That is truly an inspiring story from a stay at home mom to a world class athlete. I am sure she has even surprised herself.

Interviewer: Any last thoughts you'd like to share with us today?

Doug: Just that achievement is real for anyone to experience. The principles are simple to apply and it all begins with a desire. You have got to want to do better than you are doing now. It doesn't matter where you are at – you can always do better and dream bigger.

Those that do better and become incredibly successful are those who really recognize the importance of learning and practicing these attributes. They are proactive people who invest in their future. They are not satisfied with mediocre results. There is room at the top for everyone. These are the principles that will make your journey there easier. These are the attributes that the very most successful people I met had in common.

Interviewer: Thanks Doug for coming into the Studio today.

Doug: Thank you

Interviewer: That was Douglas Vermeeren, Author of "Amazing Success - Lessons from the most successful people I know." A brand new book that profiles lessons from more than 400 successful people from around the world. A great addition to your personal development library. For more information on this book and speaking possibilities please go to his website www.DouglasVermeeren.com or pop into your local bookstore and ask for it by name, again the title is "Amazing Success – lessons from the most successful people I know."

365 Daily lessons from

AMAZING
SUCCESS

By Douglas Vermeeren

∞ 1 ∞

Make a priority list at the end of the day for tasks to be completed for the next day. Pick the top seven things that need to be done and make sure they get done. All other emergencies and issues can then be dealt with as they come.

∞ 2 ∞

Put people first. Give respectful attention and be present even for the "little" people.

❧3❧

Get organized. If you are not organized do a little bit each day to get yourself there. Make a plan to get the future organized and start organizing your life with your plan from today onwards.

❧4❧

Dedicate 30 minutes each day to being organized.

❧ 5 ❧

Spend 30 minutes each day getting educated. It may be something that applies
directly to your field, hobbies, relationships – whatever.
Just thirst after knowledge and self improvement.

❧ 6 ❧

Find at least one person you can help significantly today.
Helping others succeed increases your own ability to succeed.

❧7❧

Plan out your day and be accountable for 15 minute increments.
Even be so bold as to plan rest time.

❧8❧

Learn to say NO.

❧ 9 ☙

Keep your commitments to a minimum and keep every commitment you make.

❧ 10 ☙

Plan to attend an event every week where you can be surrounded
by the kind of people you would like to be. Ask yourself who are they?
Where would you find them? And then get yourself there.

❧ 11 ❧

Build a good team around you that gets things done in
an ethical and effective way.

❧ 12 ❧

Ask questions from those who have already accomplished
what you are trying to do.

∼13∼

Don't be afraid to ask for help.

∼14∼

Use your resources effectively to make your time most effective.
For example:
Use the telephone first before popping in for a visit.

∼15∼

Spend less money than you make.

❧ 16 ❧

Make a budget and consider your obligations before your wants.

❧ 17 ❧

Find time to exercise, eat right and take care of your body.
It is the machine that you use in all other tasks.

❧ 18 ❧

Consider the story of the two lumberjacks who raced to cut the most wood.
One lumberjack kept stopping to take ten minute breaks, the other worked through. The lumberjack who won, was the one who stopped to take breaks.
Everyone was amazing at how this was possible .
They asked him,
"How was it possible that you beat the man who worked solidly through."
The winner replied, "I wasn't just resting, I was sharpening my saw."
Take time to sharpen your saw through education, planning and preparation.

❧19❧

Report your goals and make your self accountable.

❧20❧

Build a set of core values and beliefs that you will guide your life by.
(Some people call this a mission statement, but it needs to be deeper than just
sentences on paper.) What is your core? Really think about it.

❧21❧

Get up early and get to bed early. Morning energy is the most productive energy. Getting to bed early allows the mind to be sharp.

❧22❧

Build strong relationships instead of quick customers.
Relationships are what make for strength in business.
Russian proverb "It is better to have 100 friends than a thousand rubles."

~23~

Prioritize what matters most to occupy your time. Self and spirituality, Family, Relationships, business and then leisure time. Start with you. Remember a life guard can save no one until he knows how to swim himself.

~24~

Always strive for personal improvement. Take an inventory of what you can do better and eliminate things which you shouldn't be doing at all.

~25~

Be committed to take every worthwhile goal through to the finish line.
Can you imagine getting out of a boat before it reached the shore?
Only by sticking with something will you get the reward and
only then can a goal be called an accomplishment.

~26~

Remember there is room for everyone at the top.
Succeed as a team and remember there is enough of everything to go around.

❧27❧

Success alone is lonely. When I was in China I had the opportunity to climb one the highest peaks in the region. When I got to the top the beauty was somewhat stifled when I couldn't speak enough
Chinese to share the experience with everyone else.
To fully enjoy success you must have some one to share it with.

❧28❧

Gratitude for what we have makes us more careful with our resources.

❧29❧

Work and be busy – busy people are typically offered more because it is clear they know how to get things done.

❧30❧

Six days Shalt thou labor is also part of the fourth commandment. Do something productive, even if you aren't at work on the sixth day.

❧31❧

Failure, when learned from, is falling forward not falling down.
Learn to be resilient and do not give up when facing adversity.

❧32❧

Be cheerful and enthusiastic. An enthusiastic person with creativity is more
powerful than a less enthusiastic person with all the facts.

❧33❧

Some people talk about work, while successful people do it.
Work is the action that changes your current situation.

❧34❧

To swim far you must be in the ocean, not a swimming pool.
What you surround yourself with and where you choose to be
does make a difference.

❧35❧

Make decisions about who you are.
These decisions are the seeds of your character.
They ultimately determine who you will be.

❧36❧

Consider the marathon runner at the start of the race.
The pace they set often determines how far they will go
and how successful they will be.
Start well and start smart.

❧37❧

Do what you say you will do.

❧38❧

Be a solution oriented person. Excuses never built anything.

❧39❧

Being organized promotes clear and forward thinking.

❧40❧

The only playing field in which everyone is equal is in the amount of time we have each day. How we use our time determines our differences.
Successful people consider their use of time an investment.
Less effective people don't really think about time.
How are you investing your time?

❧41❧

It is just as important to relax properly
as it is to commitment yourself to hard work.
Consider the bow that shoots arrows.
If it is always strung tight it will soon lose its spring.
Even it needs to relax.

❧42❧

Even the best ideas without a plan often fail.

❧43❧

Making a plan and surrounding yourself with the right people is important.
Can you imagine trying to make a bridge without a blueprint?
No doubt you would never go instantly to build a bridge without a plan and
consulting proper architects and technicians.

❧44❧

It is not necessary to become perfect in a thing before you can begin to do it.
Learn as much as you can, work as hard as you can and
continue learning along the way.

❧45❧

The problem that causes most people to fail is that they give in to
procrastination and excuses.

❧46❧

Stand for something of you'll fall for anything.

❧47❧

Success is not an accident. It is a formula or a recipe.

❧48❧

How we see ourselves is a mirror of how we see our world and our possibilities.
Create a positive vision of yourself and goods things will follow.
Believe goods things will happen. Cultivate a desire to accomplish.

❧49❧

Being honest is not only reflected in what you deliver and what you say – but also in the way that you represent the truth even when words are not used.

❧50❧

How you use your time is an investment.

❧51❧

Get a mentor who can help you reach your goals and encourage you when you are struggling.

❧52❧

Be consistent and diligent until every worthwhile project or task is complete.
Starting is not enough to get to the finish line.

❧53❧

Success is not a single event but a developed habit
and series of events working together towards a destination.

54

Consider the Great Wall of China.
It is the world's largest man-made structure. However, a closer examination
would reveal that it is simply the right collection of smaller bricks.
Similarly, great people are the right combination of smaller things.

55

Don't discount the importance of a little change.
Consider a ship sailing in the Ocean.
If you change it's heading, even by a tiny degree,
it could mean arriving at an entirely different country.

❧56❧

Consider that there are many things that money cannot buy.
Money alone does not equate to success.

❧57❧

What you input into your life = the thoughts your mind produces =
Action you perform = consequences you reap.
Be aware of the kind of seeds you are planting.

✥58✥

Work smart – not just hard.

✥59✥

An important lesson in work is also knowing when to stop for the day.

✥60✥

Like a race car, we cannot perform at our maximum unless
we occasionally pull in for a pit stop and take care of ourselves.

❧ 61 ❧

The harder you work, the luckier you seem to be with accomplishing your goals. George Bernard Shaw stated once, "When I was young I observed that nine out ten things I did were failures, so I did ten times more work."

❧ 62 ❧

Success is gained by practicing and growing
our capacity to implement principles of greatness.

❧63❧

Challenges do not mean a thing is impossible – they are just a means of testing our creativity in finding a solution. Consider a mountain climber, although the peak may be in his sight he cannot always take the most direct route. Getting there often requires small deviations in your pathway to the top.

❧64❧

Communicate with those around you so they know what you are trying to do and what is expected of them.

❧65❧

Take time to enjoy relationships.
In the end they are really the most important treasure a person can possess.

❧66❧

Organize your most important tasks to be taken care of early in the day
before you are distracted with more trivial things.

❧67❧

Make a list of things that must absolutely get done for sure that day. Try and keep the list focused and to under ten items.

❧68❧

Learn to delegate as much as possible. Effective delegation includes scheduling effective reporting and follow up sessions.

✺69✺

Give more responsibility to people than what they are used to.
Treat them as more successful than what they are.
Pay them more than what they expect.
And they will work harder and be more loyal than you had imagined.

✺70✺

Remember there is always room for everyone at the top.
Scarcity thinking develops fear and greed.
Scarcity, fear and greed hinder success.

❧71❧

Treat others kindly and inspire others to greatness.

❧72❧

Put your most important tasks first in the day.
Choose your important things carefully.

❧73❧

Focus.

When you think about your plan.

Stay focused.

When you act on that plan.

❧74❧

Leaders on FIRE, INSPIRE!
Those who SIT, teach others not to give a $@#*!
(Oops - I mean... an ounce of support.)

❧75❧

Find specific ways to measure and evaluate your efforts.

❧76❧

Decide now to be more careful with the ways you spend your money.

❧77❧

Talk with mentors and peers and ask for suggestions and advice.

❧78❧

Keep a daily journal and record your thoughts and goals.

❧79❧

Spend time early in the morning in some form of meditation or prayer.
It keeps you anchored to your core.

❧80❧

Grow your education with every opportunity.

❧81❧

Don't stop when others stop. Put in more and you'll get more out.
Top sales people always contact at least 10% more people than others.

❧82❧

Set goals.
Write them down and keep them always in the forefront of your thoughts.

❧83❧

Making a plan is like constructing a blueprint.
It will not work unless you stick to it.
And if it is well thought out it will lead to the desired results.

❧84❧

Be a better listener.

❧85❧

Don't forget to reward yourself for a job well done.

❧86❧

Surround yourself with wise advisors
and consider their advice carefully with big decisions.

✥87✥

Put as many pieces in place before you begin a thing.
Think of it like trying to climb Everest.
If you showed up in only shorts
and sandals you wouldn't get very far.

≈88≈

Learn to delegate what you are not an expert in.
And make sure you delegate to good people.

≈89≈

It is better to pay more and have the job done right
than to continually backtrack to repair the same things.

≈90≈

Try to look your best.
How you look says a lot about how you conduct the other aspects of your life.

❧91❧

Be kind and courteous to others even when they are not kind to you.
Kindness changes people and you may be very surprised at the results.

❧92❧

Strive for improvement in all you do.
There is no one so good at a thing that
they cannot profit by trying to become better.

❧93❧

Follow and learn from the examples of others.
You can also learn from a bad example to be more wise.

❧94❧

Be humble when you find success. Humility is the key to continued success.

❧95❧

Stand firm in your beliefs and principles.
Don't compromise to make a quick buck.

~96~

Give back to the community and those in need.
You don't have to have great wealth to make a difference.

~97~

Smile often and mean it.

~98~

Do everything with enthusiasm and commitment. Just these two things alone will take you far in getting a job done, even if you don't begin with all the answers.

❧99❧

Have patience with the shortcomings of others and yourself.

❧100❧

Set committed written goals with fixed timelines.
Share them with a trusted friend who will follow up with you.
This is really the essence of good planning.

❧101❧

My brother and I went car shopping one day. On the lot among some exotic and luxury cars we found an old broken car. The paint was worn and it looked like it had been well used. If it had been anywhere else we would have assumed it was worthless. But among the luxury cars we automatically placed a greater value on it, assuming that it was a rare car and perhaps even a collector's edition.

Today we still don't know what make or model the car was.

But there was an interesting principle we learned that can be applied to people – surround yourself with those who are greater than you and recognized for their excellence and you will have some of it rub off on you.

❧102❧

Don't only take time to stop and smell the flowers, take time to stop and plant some. Dedicate some time and effort to making things better for those around you.

❧103❧

Don't procrastinate. Do it now.
If you don't do it now – when will you do it?

❧104❧

Set a routine that you will follow each day.
Routine and habit make progress constant.

❧105❧

Do not let trivial little things steal your time.
Focus on the big picture and do it well.
The little things will then generally take care of themselves.

❧106❧

Sit still and think about an idea.

Then once you have it, stop thinking and get to work.

Many good ideas are lost because they are never executed.

❧107❧

Learn how to dream big.

This is the key to unlocking amazing possibilities.

~108~

If you never work hard, it is impossible to stop and rest.

~109~

Life is like going up an escalator the wrong way.
If you only do what is required you stand still.
You have to work twice as hard to get ahead and go up.
And if you stand still you are falling behind.

110

Making decisions and overcoming challenges are both talents which can be learned through experience.

❧ 111 ❧

Pick your battles carefully. Some things are better left alone and will even sort themselves out. Other things require a stern unyielding stance.

❧ 112 ❧

Plan well and be sure to get your best R.O.E. – Return on your efforts.

❧ 113 ❧

The only way to move from objectives to results is effort and work.

≈114

Start. It's as simple as that!
Once you are working you can fine tune your direction to be more effective.

≈115≈

Consistently working at the right activities will generate positive results.

≈116≈

Hard work produces results. Results produce positive attitude.
Positive attitude produces excitement.
As you get excited you continue to work and the cycle continues.

❧117❧

Start with what is in your power.
Your <u>effort</u> and <u>attitude</u> are yours instantly.
Make the most of those first two things and <u>ability</u> will follow.
These are the three pillars to build success with.

❧118❧

Simply change your thoughts from "should do" to
"Will do" and you will notice amazing results.

❧119❧

Set personal daily activity quotas and meet those goals. (Ex. Set a quota for how many people you will talk to today about your business.)

❧120❧

The more you act, the less you will have to react.

❧121❧

Quality of the plan + Commitment to plan + effort = great results

❧122❧

Don't waste your time watering rocks.
Carefully find the things in your life that will grow
and water and cultivate those.

❧123❧

Success in little things leads to success in big things.

❧124❧

Ask yourself what activities and efforts in your life are best leading you to your final goal. Eliminate other things that are not worthwhile.
Remember you have the power to control what you do and do not do.

❧125❧

Find out what motivates you and reward yourself for your accomplishments.

❧126❧

Consistency in working at the right things with the right attitude
will always generate great results.

❧127❧

Spend time where you get a worthwhile return or beneficial experience.

❧128❧

Try to build where you don't have to be constantly supervising.
This allows you to build more without having to manage
what you have built so often.

❧129❧

Self management is the beginning of success.

❧130❧

Effort is more important than talent.

❧131❧

Smarten up! That's my life's motto. Learn from everything and smarten up.
The better and smarter you can do something the more effective you will be.
Always strive to find a better way.

❧132❧

Don't let yourself be satisfied with just accomplishing a task.
Seek to do your best in everything.
Soon you will find that you will attract a higher quality
and calibre of people, projects and results in your life.

❧133❧

Over delivering is the best way to eliminate competition.
Many people are naturally lazy.
If you can work harder and go the extra mile
you will go a lot further than you can imagine.

❧134❧

Time can never be bought back.
Consider carefully what you are investing your time in.
And don't let trivial things steal your time.

❧135❧

Get organized. When you are organized you can then set priorities.
Having priorities allows you to always choose to put your best foot forward.

❧136❧

Planning a day or week or even a year is like sailing a boat.
Chart your course and proceed toward your destination.
Along the way there may be minor sail or course adjustment to maximize
potential or fix a challenge. But don't lose sight of the final destination.

❧137❧

Losing focus robs many potentially successful people from reaching their goals.
The idea may have been good, they may know how to work the plan,
but lack of focus keeps them from crossing the finish line.

❧138❧

Know clearly what you want to do then be prepared to share it clearly.
Keep meetings and telephone calls short and to the point.
Talking about things too long keeps you from doing them.

❧139❧

Use the tools and people around you to overcome anything that you don't yet understand or know how to do. That's why they are called experts.
And you can't do it all.

❧140❧

Believe that you can do it.
If you don't believe you can be successful doubt
will sabotage even the best plans.

❧ 141 ❧

Put out fires quickly before they get big.

❧ 142 ❧

Double your efforts when confronted with difficult stuff.
Remember nothing is impossible. And it's moments like this that keep most people from crossing to the finish line. There is nothing so rewarding as getting through one of these moments and feeling the power of "I DID IT."

~143~

The difference between winners
and losers is how quickly they give up.

✆144✇

Successful people find a way to do it.
Others find a way out of doing it.

✆145✇

Be open to hearing criticism. Especially in business.
Those kinds of people, if listened to,
can be your most effect Business consultants.

❧146❧

If people around you can trust you to get the job done
and to do what you say you are going to do – nothing else matters.

❧147❧

The objective of my life has been to simplify things.
When things are simple I am happy.

❧148☙

Find time to dream.

Dreams, imagination and wonder are what inspire us to work harder.

Without a vision of what could be we are rarely satisfied

with where we are today.

❧149☙

Constantly strive to enhance your personal efficiency.

❧150❧

Be a constant learner and teacher to those who want to learn from you.

❧151❧

Believe that you can do anything you put your mind to, then get to work.

❧152❧

Everything you are began first as a thought in your mind.
Cultivate good thoughts and goals
and they will steer you towards better things.

❧153❧

How we solve problems will eventually dictate the kinds
of problems we experience.

❧154❧

Be a clock watcher, but let it influence you to work harder and faster.
Time moves quickly and is only available for a limited opportunity.

❧155❧

Help others around you feel safe and secure in sharing their ideas.
Let them try new ideas and experiments although they may fail.
If they fail they will come back stronger and be loyal to you
for having supported them.

～156～

Success often requires thinking outside of the box.
But don't forget that many answers
are already within the box too.
Take a look at what others are doing to be successful
and some things don't need to be reinvented.

❧157❧

Do one new thing everyday.

❧158❧

Contact and try to form business relationships with those above your comfort zone. Each step up will increase your success.

❧159❧

Find something nice to say about everyone.
Optimists attract positive energy and positive results.

❧160❧

Hang out in situations and with people that bring out the best in you.
Eliminate energy suckers and habits that hinder.

❧161❧

Believe in people and recognize and nurture the best in them.

❧162❧

Only speak kind words and always encourage those around you.

❧163❧

Leaders lead first by example and then by teaching
others how to do what they have done.

❧164❧

Success has little to do with money. It is all about relationships.
When a person has successful relationships he will be wealthy.

☙165☙

Have courage. Sharing and implementing a new idea requires courage.
Getting up after you fall requires courage.
Leading people towards the unknown requires courage.
Courage is an attribute of people who succeed, because they dare to try.

☙166☙

Don't be afraid of criticism. These people will be your most cost effective
consultants. Just be sure to consider their criticisms carefully.
Those who point out errors may not always be right.

❧ 167 ❧

Learn to communicate effectively.
If you can let people know exactly what to expect, what they will get
and when they will get it and what is required of them.
You will spare yourself many challenges.

❧ 168 ❧

Put your best foot forward. And keep walking the same way.
Give your best in everything you do.
The old adage "if it's worth doing, do it right." is true.

ᐧᒧ169ᕿ

Take notes about people around you who are doing successful things.
How are they getting there? Be aware that they have challenges too.

ᐧᒧ170ᕿ

Consider the things you enjoy doing most and reward yourself with these things
as you make your way through the things you enjoy doing least.

❧171❧

No one will ever know your bank balance when you die,
but everyone will remember how you treated people around you.
Make sure in your pursuit of financial wealth
you don't sacrifice your real legacy.

❧172❧

Determine your core values and build a firm foundation of who you are,
what you want to become and what you cherish most.

☙173☞

Prioritize your day the night before you begin it.
That way as you sleep your subconscious mind can solve many problems while
you sleep before you begin the day.

☙174☞

Use your finances with clarity.
Most people lose their financial freedom among the trivial little purchases.
Don't nickel and dime yourself away.

❧175❧

Surround yourself with people who can help you succeed.

❧176❧

Before becoming a multi-millionaire you need to become a "multi-minute-aire."
Until you learn how to maximize your time, you cannot learn how
to maximize your finances.

❧177❧

Constantly be on the look out for things that will improve your life. Absorb all the good you can and eliminate all of the non-productive negatives you can.

❧178❧

Seek out companions and associates that build people and success. Personalities and habits are contagious.

❧179❧

Find a person or a set of people that you can bounce your ideas off of.
Listen carefully as they share their ideas.

❧180❧

Find a problem and solve it.
Problem solving people become successful people.

❧ 181 ❧

Success is like a fingerprint. It is different for everyone. Take time to listen to your inner voice to find out what really makes you feel successful.

❧182❧

Grow your education by listening to and reading positive messages.
These can be found in the scriptures, inspirational books, tapes and CDs.

❧183❧

Unless you change who you are now and what you do today,
things will not be different tomorrow.

≈184≈

Take time to visualize your most successful outcomes.
Visualizing lets you see where you are headed
and you can then build your road to get there.

≈185≈

Share your needs and wants with those in your network. You'd be surprised
how many people around have the sources and resources to help you.
And they will.

✑186✑

Big things can only be accomplished by teams.

✑187✑

Don't only look for the best in other people.
Look for the best in yourself.
Look carefully and nurture it.

❧188❧

Follow the example of others who are where you want to be.
It is the difference between taking a winding road and the most direct path.
If you want to be where others are, follow their road.

❧189❧

Find a few minutes in the morning where you can meditate and sort out your first thoughts of the day. Set some quick daily goals and then begin with purpose.

❧190❧

Don't be afraid of your weaknesses.
Just find someone who can compensate and help you overcome.

❧191❧

Filter your phone calls.
Just chatting for the sake of chatting kills time.
Make your business phone calls to the point.
Consider them valuable meetings or appointments.

❧192❧

If something is not going right, look back from the beginning to figure it out.
Many times just changing your attitude
about things can change the results entirely.

❧193❧

When you think that you can do no more – go a little bit further.

❧194❧

Sometimes people don't succeed because
they don't want to recognize possibilities and they set limits.
Look around and realize that flying was impossible until someone did it.
So was the telephone, computer, TV, heart surgery and the light bulb.
Truly nothing is impossible.

❧195❧

Always be a good listener. Especially to your critics.
You never know where your next good idea will come from.

≈196≈

Be innovative and fresh. It's okay to say ~ why reinvent the wheel?
But you should always find a different way to drive the cart.

≈197≈

Set goals for things you wish to accomplish in every meeting you are involved in
whether in person or on the phone. Meetings without purpose tend to be
longer than they need to be and most times are much less effective.

❧198❧

Businesses, partnerships and relationships endure when we think of solutions and scenarios that benefit everyone.

❧199❧

Consider when you fill your car with gas. You can only go so far and do so many things. How you use your assets is like filling your car with gas too. You must choose where you will go with your resources. And when you are empty you are empty. It is impossible to drive further than your gas. But while you can drive you can do many things. One of them of course will be to go and get more gas so you can keep going. Some people also spend their whole life driving to the park instead of driving to work.

✇200✇

Money is not the only resource to be wise with. But money can quickly hinder all of the other resources when you don't know how to manage it.

✇201✇

Cultivate and care for your relationships.
Relationships are the hub of other things.

❧202❧

Information and education are among the greatest advantages you can attain.
While it is true people may have natural skills and talents – education and
information are the elements that put you in the right position
to use those gifts to their maximum.

❧203❧

Only by looking at the end of the course
can you actually begin to plan your route.

❧204❧

Even the best athlete will fail if he is not part of a winning team.

❧205❧

To exceed at a game you must understand the game
and always strive to be better.
The same is true in business and life.

❧206❧

Be focused. Where you focus is where you will arrive.
If a race car driver is looking at the wall on a corner that is what he will hit.
If he stays focused on keeping the car in control
and keeps his eyes on the road that is where he will go.

❧207❧

Sometimes you have to just forget that a thing
seems impossible and find a way to do it.

~208~

Build a strong team around you. When there is something you cannot do, find others with the talents to get the job done right.

~209~

Learn to identify the real problem rather than just a hiccup or something that will just require hard work.

✌210✍

Finding a win/win deal works for everybody, but I try to find a way to give just a little more to the other guy. When I do this I often find that I win big in building and keeping the relationship strong.

✌211✍

Watch other successful people and try
and emulate their best traits and their habits that make them successful.

❧212☙

Keep positive. One of the major areas an entrepreneur neglects when starting a new venture is to take an emotional inventory regularly. New businesses are full of ups, as the deals get done, and downs when they experience a week with little money. It can make a person near crazy.
Understand that these ups and downs will occur.

❧213☙

Don't be afraid – get prepared.

❧214❧

Failure, disappointment, critics and other challenges will all be fond memories
once you persevere and get the job done.
Fear takes a person's eyes off his goal.

❧215❧

How you think determines your outcome. Think big and you will be big.

❧216❧

Envision possibilities and then build those possibilities in reality.

❧217❧

Act as though you are already the kind of person you
want to be and eventually you will be that person.

❧218❧

Continually push yourself beyond your comfort zone
in all areas of your life and business.
When you have a moment of fear, instead of thinking – ouch be careful.
Think Wow! Opportunity to excel.

❧219❧

Become a better listener.

Most people are ready to help you if you give them a chance to tell you about it.

❧220❧

Associate with the very best people you can surround yourself with.

Success is contagious.

≈221≈

If you are in sales think of yourself as an educator not a salesperson. Learn as many skills to educate. This will help you share your message and when people understand your message and how it can benefit them, the sales process becomes easy and natural.

≈222≈

Learn how to handle stress.
Recognize it for what it is and really how temporary it is.

❧223❧

Commit to doing everything excellent.

❧224❧

Life gets better only by seeking out good and better things and eliminating things that are negative and suck energy away. Be proactive and become a seeker of the best things in yourself and others.

❧225❧

Obtain as much education as possible.

❧226❧

Focus on relationships first.

❧227❧

Take some time away from work to recharge.
Many people leave work to go home and work some more. Don't do this.
Recharging is essential to being more productive the next day.

❧228❧

Establish a vision of where you are heading and then don't let little challenges take that that vision away. Focus on the big picture.

❧229❧

Keep a journal. It helps you to sort out your thoughts and challenges.
It also lets you see where you have been
and what you have been able to accomplish so far.
(And then when it's time to write your biography you're already almost done.)

❧230❧

Avoid scarcity thinking.
Remember there is always more
than enough for everyone.
And you also attract what you think about most.

~231~

Get up earlier and spend time developing yourself in a new area.

~232~

Prepare more carefully for every meeting you have.
Make a list of objectives you hope to accomplish and then within the meetings design a strategy to follow up.

❧233❧

All good things started as an idea. Take time to just think about ideas.
Ideas of how you can be better, have better relationships, make your business
better and find better solutions everywhere in your life.

❧234❧

Balance your life with the arts.
Go and enjoy the talents of others.

❧235❧

There really aren't any short cuts to success, because it is not a destination.
Success is a journey. Success is an act of becoming.
This is an internal exercise. It is already within you. The more focused and
committed you are to becoming the kind of person you want to be the easier it
will be for you to feel successful.

❧236❧

Visualize yourself succeeding.
The more focused and real this vision is the
more likely it is that you will be able to attain it.

∞237∞

Learn to sort your problems into categories. 1) Do something about it now. 2) Leave it alone. 3) Can't do anything about it – so don't worry about it. Some problems require attention. Some will go away on their own. Others won't change no matter what you do. If you can divide these effectively and deal with them in appropriate ways you will find life becomes easier.

∞238∞

Become an expert in your field.

❧239❧

Act with purpose. Act quickly.
You can't succeed by staying exactly where you are.

❧240❧

Become likeable.
When you are likeable others are interested to help you succeed also.

❧241❧

Be a good listener and treat everyone as important.

❧242❧

Do twice as much today as you did yesterday.

❧243❧

Set goals.
Write them down in clarity and attach a date and plan for their accomplishment.

❧244❧

Have a weekly planning meeting with yourself.
In the meeting look at your past week and your coming week
and set goals as to how you can become more effective.

❧245❧

Look for sincere reasons to praise people around you.

❧246❧

Consider what aspects of your life are slowing you down.
(ie. Your ability to manage time, your paperwork organization, your sales skills,
too much time in travel – whatever it may be) Write it down and make a plan of
action on how to strengthen yourself in that area
or make better use of the obstacle.

❧247❧

Learn to think on paper. Write down your ideas, goals and plans. The mere act
of writing them down allows them to be considered more carefully
and you always have a record of good ideas.

❧248❧

Focus on your goal or you will diffuse the energy needed to get there.

❧249❧

You want to change your situation? Ask the Chemical question today – WW H2 HSN – What Would Have 2 Happen starting Now?

❧250❧

Remember all successful people started out just like anyone else and all successful people still have problems.

They are not super heroes – they are other humans who have simply learned lessons that have helped them to build their life differently.

❧251❧

Winners make progress, Whiners make excuses.

≈252≫

Everything counts.

≈253≫

Successful people learn how to prioritize and put first things first.

≈254≫

Sometimes it is better to just walk away from a deal.

❧255❧

Make every hour count.

❧256❧

While you are supposed to be working if you find yourself involved in an activity
that is wasting time or non-productive – stop.

Make every moment an investment in your future.

Top people look for ways to make every moment productive.

❧257❧

Don't get discouraged when you fail.
It will happen often as you learn to become better.
Remember it is a process.

❧258❧

Do something everyday that moves you toward your major goals.

❧259❧

To obtain any end result you must pay the price.
The reason most people don't succeed is that they aren't sure what
the "price" is exactly. We are already all paying something into
something – even those who aren't doing well are paying a price that
life exacts of them for their choices.

So the answer to success is to be proactive and find out the real
price and then adjust our lives to start paying it.

❧260❧

Act instead of being acted upon.

❧261❧

Sometimes you have to do things you don't like
to do to be able to get to the things that you do like.

~262~

Life is like a funnel.   At first we have great freedom and then life restricts us based on the choices we have made. If we have made good choices we can go through the funnel without much resistance to experience unlimited freedom.

If we have made poor choices we cannot go through the funnel so easily,
and in some cases not at all.
Often times the consequences of our choices require us to back up,
fix something that will now allow us to be fluid,
then we can move on to unlimited freedom.

❧263❧

Successful people are both teachers and students.

❧264❧

Solve your problems. All problems originate at some source with people.
Sometimes we have to ask for help and many problems can be healed by just
becoming a better listener and becoming genuinely interested.

❧265❧

Be persistent. Anything really worth doing often takes more than one try.

266

Be a motivator of people, not a downer.

267

Don't forget to celebrate good things that happen.

268

Form alliances and relationships with other businesses.
Not only those that can help you, but also those you can help.
Good relationships are mostly about what you can give.

∾269∾

Be a possibility thinker.

∾270∾

All good things start with good and positive thoughts.

∾271∾

Define success in terms of feelings, relationships, security and serviceability –
rather than by the accumulation of things.

❧272❧

Do nice things for people without telling them
and without expecting anything in return.

❧273❧

Learn to delegate where you can.

❧274❧

Learn this one solution: hard work.

❧275❧

Avoid detours of the day. Make a plan and stick to it.

❧276❧

Don't sweat yesterday – you can't do much about it. It's like trying to drive a car by looking through the rear view mirror. Focus on what can be done better today and take advantage of opportunities to build a stronger future.

~277~

Successful people put family first.

~278~

A skill is learned in the practicing of it.
Remember that no skill is attained with perfection instantly.
New attributes take time to develop.

❧279❧

Nothing is without consequence. Whether you do it or not there will be a result as a consequence of the action or inaction you have chosen to take.

❧280❧

Your results will be equal to your efforts. However, significant and well thought out initial effort can pay dividends long after the efforts have ceased.

❧281❧

Have a definite plan and goal – coasting along and making it up as you go is like trying to sail a ship without a rudder.

❧282❧

Read one self improvement or business development article each day.

❧283❧

Spend most of your time planning it and organizing it and then the rest of your time getting it done. Planning it right results in building it right.

❧284❧

Learn how to put your efforts in appropriate places. Remember the concept that 80% of your business will come from 20% of your customers. Find that 20%.

❧285☙

Studies have shown that our mind often places incidents we vividly and carefully imagine as genuine experience, both in terms of trauma and victory.

Invest time to imagine and create
an experience of success in your mind.

❧286❧

Take personal responsibility. Winners find solutions, losers cling to excuses.

❧287❧

Don't just listen to good advice.
Apply it directly to something you are currently doing.
Advice and lessons are of no value unless you implement them.

❧288❧

Remember that just because you don't see instant results
it does not mean you are not making progress.

❧289❧

Problems cannot be solved at the same level of thinking
as when you created them.

❧290❧

Ask for help when you need it.

❧291❧

Break down big jobs into little tasks.

❧292❧

Try and anticipate challenges, obstacles and opportunities
and then position yourself to be ready.

❧293❧

Recognize that you have power to make changes to any situation.

✑294✑

All the seeds of success are within us.
The only thing we must do is nurture them.

✑295✑

Pick one thing to develop and work on in ourselves each day.

✑296✑

Don't ever settle for less than your best.

❧297❧

Dress for success. The way we dress often determines how we feel.
Have you ever considered how a Halloween costume or a Santa Claus suit
changes how we behave? If we dress successfully we feel differently.

❧298❧

Take care of your body and your mind.
Both require exercise and begin with stretching.

❧299❧

Focus your energies where you get your major results.

❧300❧

Finish major projects before beginning to create others. One of the attributes of the least successful people I've met is that they always have lots of amazing things in development. Pick one and get it done.

❧301❧

Spend your most productive hours involved in your most effective activities.

❧302❧

Review your core values often to keep your perspective about why you are doing what you do each day.

❧303❧

Don't be afraid to consider and try new ideas.

❧304❧

Ask someone who knows nothing about your business,
"How clear is my message?" and "can you think of a better way to tell my story?"
You will be surprised at some of the insights you will gain.

❧305❧

Be clear about what you want and are trying to do.
Start in your own mind and carry this into your communication with others.

❧306❧

Preparation is the mark of a professional.
"Winging it." mentality always creates "Winging it" results.

❧307❧

Measure your performance through
the use of journals and regular personal inventory.

❧308❧

Allocate your work time carefully. Spend it in the most productive areas.

❧309❧

Don't live in your comfort zone. Live a few feet outside of it. Comfort does not provide an environment for growth.

❧310❧

Identify one key challenge in your life or business and then focus on finding a solution. Once you have conquered this one, find another one to eliminate.

∽311∾

Don't ever let rejection or critics slow you down.
Remember that rejection statements are often just feelings expressed by someone who wishes they had the courage to do what you are doing.

∽312∾

You determine your possibilities by what you do with your present.

∽313∾

You can if you believe you can.

~314~

Begin your day with an organizational meeting with yourself.

~315~

Decide to do your very best in everything you do.

~316~

Recognize there are no limits to what you can achieve.

✎317✎

Character comes from your habits. Habits come from what you do.
What you do comes from what you think about. Guard your thoughts.

✎318✎

Be 100% present when you are meeting with people.

✎319✎

Spend time and participate in activities in the circles
of those you wish to be like.

❧320❧

Remember that as a member of the human species you have the same potential
as all other members of our race born on this planet.
The only difference is found in the choices we make moment by moment.

❧321❧

Compensation is often equal to contribution.
If you want great things you need to contribute great things.

❧322❧

Keep your eye on the end goal.
Don't let short term set backs blind you from possibilities.

❧323❧

Learn to be thankful and express gratitude often.

❧324❧

What can you do differently right now to get better results?

❧325❧

Remember you are as unique as your own finger print.
There are gifts that you have that will make you more successful in your area
than anyone who has come before you.

❧326❧

Learn to ask good questions and become a great listener.

❧327❧

Try to always be relaxed, cheerful, delightful and positive.
Panic and chaos are counter productive to success.

❧328❧

When you commit to show up – do so and with your best efforts.

❧329❧

Never bite off more than you can chew and swallow with ease.

❧330❧

Be busy when its time to work.
When you stop to rest it is hard to get started again.

❧331❧

Learn new skills and tools each day.

❧332❧

Strive for excellence even in the little things you do.

❧333❧

Solve problems as you encounter them.

❧334❧

Keep in contact with your most important opportunities
and clients daily where possible.

❧335❧

Build and focus on quality business opportunities
rather than quantity opportunities.

❧336❧

Be ever present in relationships.
This starts with genuine listening.

❧337❧

Always complete your tasks and duties on time.

❧338❧

Be a master of your money. Not the other way around.

﹏339﹏
Think Big!

❧340❧

Have a plan <u>and</u> a destination.

❧341❧

Remember that procrastination is the biggest thief of all time.

❧342❧

Get with the right crowd!

❧343❧

Strive for personal improvement!

❧344❧

Smile and don't let stress run your life.

∼345∼

Good input = good output.

∼346∼

Make time to enjoy the little things in life.
Remember that most often the little things are the most important.

❧347❧

Always perform your duties as though you really need a letter of recommendation from the person you are working with. Because the truth is you will always get it through word of mouth or one way or another.

❧348❧

When things go wrong return to your core values
and they will help you solve problems effectively.

❧349❧

When people are comparing apples and oranges, deliver them a banana.

Find a way to stand out and make people take notice.

The every day stuff is always forgotten.

Uniqueness always leaves a mark.

❧350❧

Be confident.

Even when you don't have all the answers, confidence can go a long way.

❧351❧

Good music, exercise, service for others and comedy can alter your mood instantly. Keep some of these tools handy for when you hit speed bumps that get you feeling less than great.

❧352❧

Start the day right and most of the rest of it will follow

≈353≈

Make a list of personal attributes you would like to attain.
Then make a plan of things you can do right now to begin to develop them.

≈354≈

Make a list of purposes behind your daily activities and meetings.

≈355≈

Under promise, over deliver.

❧356❧

Invest your working time into things that pay a return on your efforts.

❧357❧

Set aside a budget just for personal development and education.

❧358❧

Eliminate time wasters from your day. (These can include travel time, time between appointments, meetings that can be done by phone, etc.)

❧359❧

Learn to save. Invest what you save. Get your money working for you.

❧360❧

Eat a proper diet. Get enough sleep. Your body is your tool.

❧361❧

Prepare ahead of time for meetings and appointments
so that you can focus on the task at hand.

❧362❧

Take time off occasionally just to be by yourself to reset your core.

❧363❧

Keep a record of your hours – even if you work for yourself.
When you have accountability you begin to take
more care of how you spend your time.

❧364❧

Reward yourself for work that you do well.

❦365❧

Knowing the right answers is not enough.
You must DO what you know.

About the Author

Douglas Vermeeren is a Top International Speaker and Author on turning Human Potential into Amazing Performance. In 1995 Avenue Magazine voted Doug one of the Top ten Calgarians to watch.

He was the first North American to ever address the Chinese Political Party and Education Leaders on Performance and Motivation. He was officially awarded the distinction of visiting Professor by the Wu Zhai University. Since then he has spoken on nearly every continent on the globe.

Doug has been published in 22 languages worldwide and has been featured on National TV, Radio and Print.

Currently Doug lives in Canada with his wife Holly. They have three children. Julienne, Jordan and Jared.

You can find out more about Doug at www.DouglasVermeeren.com

Turn Your Amazing Potential into Awesome Performance!!!

Learn how to take your **Amazing Potential** and turn it into…

Amazing Possibility, and then build that into…

an **Amazing Probability,** which in turn can become your own personal…

Amazing Performance!

Doug Vermeeren has given these "accelerated achievement" tools and "Power Performance" tips to Top achievers around the world.

Why not get Doug to come and give your team the same tools?

Douglas Vermeeren can be contacted for speaking engagements through his website.

www.DouglasVermeeren.com

The DJV companies

Business Boost
Business Boost hosts a variety of speaking events through out the world.
These speaking events feature top speakers in the field of personal development.
If you want to find the next event coming to your area go to www.BusinessBoostExpertEvents.com

Business Boost SUCCESS
Business Boost SUCCESS develops Coaches, speakers and personal development trainers through out the world. The Business Boost programs are calculated to turn the average coach in the crowd into an enthusiastic expert. You can find out more at www.BusinessBoostSUCCESS.com

Business Boost Publishing
Each year Business Boost Publishing releases several compilation books featuring top experts on subjects such as personal development, investing, organization, achievement and more!
Go to www.BusinessBoostSUCCESS.com to find more information.

All Human beings have Amazing Potential!

Want to learn how to capture yours?

Also available from Douglas Vermeeren at most fine bookstores:

Books
Amazing Success – Lessons from the Most Successful people I know
365 Daily Lessons from Amazing Success
Accelerated Achievement (Expanded tools set)

Audio recordings
Amazing Possibilities – Special interview CD
Are you An Expert? Especially for Coaches and Speakers
Accelerated Achievement – Get to your goals instantly!

You can also find these online at www.DouglasVermeeren.com

Want more <u>FREE</u> tips and articles for Top Achievers?

Send an e-mail to:
Topachiever@DouglasVermeeren.com